Settler Colonialism

Roxanne Dunbar-Ortiz

Daraja Press

Published by Daraja Press
https://darajapress.com

ISBN: 9781990263507

© 2022, 2021 Roxanne Dunbar-Ortiz

Cover design: Kate McDonnell

Series: Thinking Freedom
Series editor: Firoze Manji

Library and Archives Canada Cataloguing in Publication

Title: Settler colonialism / Roxanne Dunbar-Ortiz.
Names: Dunbar-Ortiz, Roxanne, 1938- author.
Description: Series statement: Thinking freedom | Excerpt from "Not A Nation of Immigrants: Settler Colonialism, White Supremacy, and a History of Erasure and Exclusion (2021). | Includes bibliographical references.
Identifiers: Canadiana 20220255679 | ISBN 9781990263507 (softcover)
Subjects: LCSH: Settler colonialism—United States.
Classification: LCC E179.5 .D86 2022 | DDC 973.3—dc23

CONTENTS

Introduction

Settler Colonialism examines the genesis in the USA of the first full-fledged settler state in the world, which went beyond its predecessors in 1492 Iberia and British-colonized Ireland with an economy based on land sales and enslaved African labor, an implementation of the fiscal-military state. Both the liberal and the rightwing versions of the national narrative misrepresent the process of European colonization of North America. Both narratives serve the critical function of preserving the "official story" of a mostly benign and benevolent USA as an anticolonial movement that overthrew British colonialism. The pre-US independence settlers were colonial settlers just as they were in Africa and India or like the Spanish in Central and South America. The nation of immigrants myth erases the fact that the United States was founded as a settler state from its inception and spent the next hundred years at war against the Native Nations in conquering the continent. Buried beneath the tons of propaganda—from the landing of the English "pilgrims" (Protestant Christian evangelicals) to James Fenimore Cooper's phenomenally popular The Last of the Mohicans claiming settlers' "natural rights" not only to the Indigenous peoples' territories but also to the territories claimed by other European powers—is the fact that the founding of the United States created a division of the Anglo empire, with the US becoming a parallel empire to Great Britain, ultimately overcoming it. From day one, as was specified in the Northwest Ordinance, which preceded the US Constitution, the new "republic for empire," as Thomas Jefferson called the new United States, envisioned the future shape of what is now the forty-eight states of the continental US. The founders drew up rough maps, specifying the first territory to conquer as the "Northwest Territory." That territory was the Ohio Valley and the Great Lakes region, which was already populated with Indigenous villages and farming communities thousands of years old. Even before independence, mostly Scots Irish settlers had seized Indigenous farmlands and hunting grounds in the Appalachians and are revered historically as first settlers and rebels, who in the mid-twentieth century began claiming indigeneity. Self-indigenizing by various groups of settlers is a recurrent theme in story of settler colonialism, white supremacy, and the history of erasure and exclusion about which I have written elsewhere.[1]

---

[1] Roxanne Dunbar-Ortiz, Not "a nation of immigrants" : Settler Colonialism, White Supremacy, and a History of Erasure and Exclusion (Boston: Beacon Press, 2021)

Settler colonialism:
"A structure, not an event"

As the late Patrick Wolfe emphasized in his groundbreaking research, settler colonialism is a structure, not an event.[1] Wolfe was an Australian anthropologist and historian, one of the initial theorists and historians of settler colonialism. He researched, wrote, taught, and lectured internationally on race, colonialism, Indigenous peoples' and Palestinian histories, imperialism, genocide, and critical history of anthropology. He was also a human rights activist who used his scholarship and voice to support the rights of oppressed peoples.

But in the case of the United States, settler colonialism was more than a colonial structure that developed and replicated itself over time in the 170 years of British colonization in North America preceding the founding of the United States. The founders were not an oppressed, colonized people. They were British citizens being restrained by the monarch from expanding the thirteen colonies to enrich themselves. They were imperialists who visualized the conquest of the continent and gaining access to the Pacific and China. Achieving that goal required land, wealth, and settler participation. They devised a unique plan, manifest in the 1787 Northwest Ordinance, which was created during the War of Independence by the Continental Congress and reenacted at independence by the US Congress in 1789. Designed as what historian Howard Lamar called "an internal colonial system for the West," its provisions were borrowed in part from the British system of settler colonialism in Ulster, Ireland, and the thirteen North American colonies. However, this invention was something new, the constitutional construction of the fiscal-military settler state, with both ethnic cleansing of the Native presence and chattel slavery producing racial capitalism.

The Northwest Ordinance provided for eventual settler self-government once European American settlers outnumbered the Indigenous population. This land act guaranteed to the settlers property, civil rights, religious freedom, trial by jury, representational legislation, and public education. That ultimate conclusion, however, was preceded by successive stages of colonial development, from military ethnic cleansing and control to a federally appointed territorial government to a semi-representational government to, finally, admission into the United States as a state. This constituted a unit of the fiscal-military nation-state. Lamar observes that apologists for US expansionism do not see the ordinance as a reflection of colonialism but rather as a means of "reconciling the problem of liberty with the problem of empire."[2] The founders were unapologetic imperialists, chips off the old block of British imperialism, but with the added conceit of an "empire for liberty," as Thomas Jefferson conceived the future. Historian David Reynolds writes that Jefferson believed the US empire was destined to assume the responsibility to spread freedom around the world, starting with the North American continent and intervening abroad. US foreign policy was stamped with this concept and has provided the ideological motivation for all US wars and interventions.[3]

Through the Northwest Ordinance, the United States created a unique land system among colonial powers, including Britain. In the US system, land itself—not just what was produced from the land, such as agriculture, mining, logging, grazing, and so on—was the most important exchange commodity for the accumulation of capital and building the national treasury. In order to comprehend the apparently irrational genocidal policy of the US government toward the presence of Native nations on the land, the centrality of land sales in building the economic base of the US capitalist system must be the frame of reference. This policy was embedded in the design of the fiscal-military state. As Wolfe summed up the issue,

> Tribal land was tribally-owned—tribes and private property did not mix. Indians were the original communist menace Whatever settlers may say—and they generally have a lot to say—the primary motive for elimination is not race (or religion, ethnicity, grade of civilization, etc.) but access to territory. Territoriality is settler colonialism's specific, irreducible element.[4]

However, Wolfe didn't quite understand the difference for the US founders between territory and land and the centrality of land as real estate, but he makes a correct point about US American obsession with private property. Regarding the communal nature of Native societies, Senator Henry Dawes, arguing in the 1880s for allotment of collectively held Indigenous lands, said,

> The defect of the [reservation] system was apparent. It is Henry George's system and under that there is no enterprise to make your home any better than that of your neighbors. There is no selfishness, which is at the bottom of civilization. Till this people will

consent to give up their lands, and divide among their citizens so that each can own the land he cultivates they will not make much more progress.5

Private property on steroids

Although private property in land had long been a fact of life in Europe, it was demarcated by the contour of streams, rivers, tree lines, rock formations, and mountains and was reserved for the economic and political elite. The United States, being founded as a settler-colonial, fiscal-military state, created something new under the sun, the plat system of privatizing land into marketable units. The Northwest Ordinance spawned the Public Land Survey System (PLSS), a unique surveying method to plat, that is, divide land, transforming it into property for sale and settling, plots of 160 acres with sections of four plots, or 640 acres. As the US took more land with the Louisiana Purchase, the Oregon Territory, and half of México, the government promised "free land" to Europeans and European Americans for the purpose of recruiting and motivating settlers to squat on Indigenous peoples' lands. With Indigenous resistance to the squatters, the army would be dispatched.[6] The pieces of paper, deeds representing units of land, made up the commodity market that built the United States capitalist system and remains its central factor. The other main commodity until 1860 was human, the enslaved African body with its deed of sale.Historian Donald Harman Akenson aptly describes the implementation of the Land Ordinance:

> Its importance was equal to that of the trumpet-toned Constitution of 1787. It did not deal with ethereal concepts such as the pursuit of happiness but

instead declared in practical terms how the land from the Appalachian Mountains up to the Mississippi River was to be conquered. This was to be done by surveyors' chains, each twenty-two yards in length. The measuring began at an arbitrary point in the Ohio Territory, and invisible lines were drawn on the land to form a grid of perfect rectangles marked by cairns, iron bars, and the occasional brass plate cemented onto a masonry base. Each of the rectangles had its own map reference, and as the U.S. imperium expanded, the grid eventually reached the Pacific coast and stretched between Mexico and British North America. The lines on the land not only conquered natural topography but also made possible the liberation of parcels of land from their previous occupants and their efficient allocation to newcomers.7

This was the implementation of the fiscal-military state, the state made for war in order to appropriate property.

From the beginning of surveys in the newly claimed Northwest Territory to the Pacific Ocean, the lands claimed by the surveys were already populated with Indigenous peoples, but the land was treated as *terra nullius*, unpopulated land, while the Indigenous nations and communities, reduced in numbers by genocidal warfare that caused displacement, starvation, crowded refugee situations, and resultant infectious diseases, were forced onto army-guarded reservations, dependent on government rations. The Indigenous peoples of the large Native agricultural nations of the South were forcibly relocated to west of the Mississippi. This is important for understanding not only how settler colonialism defines the United States and all its institutions, but also, as Mahmood Mamdani has documented, that "all of the defining institutions of settler colonialism as practiced in the nineteenth, twentieth, and twenty-first centuries were first developed in North America. The US tribal homeland was the prototype not only for the South African reserve but also the Nazi concentration camp."8

Free-Soiler imperialism

During the Civil War, President Abraham Lincoln did not forget his Free-Soiler base who brought him to that high office. "Free-soil" meant free of chattel slavery for white commercial farmers, like Lincoln's family, who could not afford to purchase enslaved bodies. Congress, at Lincoln's behest, passed the Homestead Act in 1862, as well as the Morrill Act, the latter transferring large tracts of Indigenous land to the states to establish land grant universities. The Pacific Railroad Act provided private companies with nearly two hundred million acres of Indigenous land.9 With these massive land grabs, the US government broke multiple treaties with Indigenous nations whose people were still living there. It would take genocidal military force to evict them. Most of the western territories, including Colorado, North and South Dakota, Montana, Washington, Idaho, Wyoming, Utah, New México, and Arizona, were delayed in achieving statehood, because Indigenous nations resisted appropriation of their lands and outnumbered the settlers—until they didn't. So, the colonization plan for the West established during the Civil War was carried out over the following three decades of war and land grabs.

Under the Homestead Act, 1.5 million homesteads were granted to settlers west of the Mississippi, comprising nearly three hundred million acres (a half million square miles) taken from the Indigenous collective estates and privatized for the market. The dispersal of landless settler populations from east of the Mississippi served as an "escape valve" for the ruling class, lessening the likelihood of class conflict as the Industrial Revolution accelerated the use of cheap immigrant labor. Little of the land appropriated under the Homestead Act was distributed to actual single-family homesteaders. It was passed instead to large operators or land speculators. The land laws appeared to have been created for that result. An individual could acquire 1,120 or more acres of land, even though homestead and preemption (legalized squatting) claims were limited to 160 acres.[10] A claimant could obtain a homestead and secure title after five years or pay cash within six months. Then he could acquire another 160 acres under preemption by living on another piece of land for six months and paying $1.25 per acre. While acquiring these titles, he could also be fulfilling requirements for a timber culture claim of 160 acres and a desert land claim of 640 acres, neither of which required occupancy for title. Other men within a family or other partners in an enterprise could take out additional desert land claims to increase their holdings even more. As industrialization quickened, land as a commodity—"real estate"—remained the basis of the US economy and capital accumulation.[11]

The federal land grants to the railroad barons—carved out of Indigenous territories—were not limited to the width of the railroad tracks, but rather formed a checkerboard of square-mile sections stretching for hundreds of miles on both sides of the right of way. This was land the railroads were free to sell to settlers in parcels for their own profit. The 1863–1864 federal banking acts mandated a national currency, chartered banks, and permitted the government to guarantee bonds. As war profiteers, financiers, and industrialists such as John D. Rockefeller, Andrew Carnegie, and J. P. Morgan used these laws to amass wealth in the East, Leland Stanford, Collis P. Huntington, Mark Hopkins, and Charles Crocker in the West grew rich from building railroads with cheap Chinese and Irish labor and eastern capital on land granted by the US government.[12]

Settler colonialism as genocide

The history of the United States is a history of settler colonialism. The objective of settler colonialism is to terminate Indigenous peoples as nations and communities with land bases in order to make the land available to European settlers. Extermination and assimilation are the methods used. This is the very definition of genocide. The word and its definition were created by Raphael Lemkin in 1944, published in his book Axis Rule in Occupied Europe.[13]

Lemkin was Polish, of Jewish descent, and a respected lawyer and prosecutor in Poland until the 1939 German invasion. Although Lemkin escaped to Sweden, forty-nine of his relatives perished in the Holocaust. Lemkin became an advisor to the chief counsel of the Nuremberg trials, during which his concept of genocide as a crime in international law did not yet exist and was not one of the legal bases for the trials. Then, for two years, with the support of the Truman administration, Lemkin lobbied the member states of the new United Nations to adopt the Genocide Convention, which the General Assembly did in the same session as the passage of the Declaration on Human Rights. "Genocide" is a legal term with a precise definition, enshrined in the international treaty the United Nations Convention on the Prevention and Punishment of the Crime of Genocide, presented in 1948 and adopted in 1951. Although President Truman signed the convention, it went into effect in the United States only in 1988 when the US Congress finally ratified it, the only member state of the United Nations that had not done so.

The convention is not retroactive, so the United States is not liable under the Genocide Convention before 1988. The Truman administration had lobbied in favor of it at the United Nations, and President Truman signed the Convention and sent it to the Senate for ratification. There, the all-white Senate expressed concern that genocide charges might result from the history of racial segregation, lynching, and Ku Klux Klan activities. In addition, although the treaty was not retroactive, senators expressed fear that it would be used to define the nineteenth-century US treatment of Native Americans as genocide. As the senators feared, in 1951, the Civil Rights Congress, led by the cofounder of the National Association for the Advancement of Colored People (NAACP) W. E. B. Du Bois and the opera star Paul Robeson, filed a petition in the United Nations titled *We Charge Genocide: The Historic Petition to the United Nations for Relief from a Crime of the United States Government Against the Negro People*, in which they stated:

> Out of the inhuman black ghettos of American cities, out of the cotton plantations of the South, comes this record of mass slayings on the basis of race, of lives deliberately warped and distorted by the willful creation of conditions making for premature death, poverty and disease. It is a record that calls aloud for condemnation, for an end to these terrible injustices that constitute a daily and ever-increasing violation of the United Nations Convention on the Prevention and Punishment of the Crime of Genocide.[14]

Thereafter, when ratification would be proposed in the Senate, similar, more nuanced, arguments would be aired. They included the possibility that the actions of the US military in Korea and Vietnam might be cause for a genocide charge. Native American intellectuals and scholars of the 1950s onward also discussed the possibilities of international human rights law, and after the US signed the Genocide Convention in 1988, work on developing cases began. Finally, pressure on the Reagan administration by the Jewish and Armenian lobbies broke the US holdout. But by that time, the radical civil rights and Black Power movements had waned and dispersed, and even when a movement for reparations for slavery developed in the 1990s, the Genocide Convention was not referenced.

Challenging Native American discussions and publications, especially since the 1992 Columbian quincentenary, US historians and other mainstream scholars and intellectuals, including some human rights activists, have exerted considerable energy in attempting to redefine the Genocide Convention in ways that conclude that it in no way applies to the United States either historically or currently. But the Genocide Convention is not a complex document for which the meaning can easily be misinterpreted, and its terms align with US policies and actions.[15] In the convention, any one of five acts can be considered genocide if "committed with intent to destroy, in whole or in part, a national, ethnic, racial or religious group."

These acts are:

- Killing members of the group
- Causing serious bodily or mental harm to members of the group

- Deliberately inflicting on the group conditions of life calculated to bring about its physical destruction in whole or in part
- Imposing measures intended to prevent births within the group
- Forcibly transferring children of the group to another group . . .

The followings acts are punishable:

- Genocide
- Conspiracy to commit genocide
- Direct and public incitement to commit genocide
- Attempt to commit genocide
- Complicity in genocide

The 1951 Civil Rights Congress petition *We Charge Genocide* pointed out:

> It is sometimes incorrectly thought that genocide means the complete and definitive destruction of a race or people. The Genocide Convention, however, . . . defines genocide as any killings on the basis of race, or, in its specific words, as "killing members of the group." Any intent to destroy, in whole or in part, a national, racial, ethnic or religious group is genocide, according to the Convention. Also, the Convention states, "causing serious bodily or mental harm to members of the group," is genocide as well as "killing members of the group."[16]

The analytical tools provided by the Genocide Convention are essential for historical investigations into the effects of

European and European American colonialism, particularly settler colonialism, which led to the establishment of the United States and was inherently committed to elimination of the Indigenous nations, but also including the transatlantic slave trade, slavery, the situation of descendants of enslaved Africans, and the annexation of half of México and the treatment of Mexicans. But most important, the Genocide Convention is applicable to US policies and actions since 1988, when the United States ratified the convention. There is no statute of limitations.

The term "genocide," both in popular use and often by historians and other scholars, even legal scholars, is often misused to indicate only extreme examples of mass murder, the death of vast numbers of people, as in the Holocaust, or in the midst of aggressive warfare, as, for instance, in Cambodia, thereby dismissing Native and African American claims of US genocide. What is important—and no doubt surprising to many—is that the United Nations' organized war crimes tribunal did not prosecute the Khmer Rouge's mass killings of hundreds of thousands of Cambodians, the ethnic Khmer who comprised the majority of the population and the largest number of victims, for genocide. The specific charges of genocide-related solely to the Khmer Rouge's actions against one Indigenous group, the Cham, and to the ethnic Vietnamese population, who were also targeted for elimination because they were not Khmer. Lars Olsen, the tribunal's legal communications officer, explains that is because the definition of genocide in law "is different from what many people would regard as genocide." Simply put, the 1948 Genocide Convention defines genocide as having the intention to eliminate, in part or in full, a group of people based on their race, religion, ethnicity or nationality, and need not be accompanied by warfare, therefore not in the category of war crimes *per se*.[17]

The Khmer Rouge slaughter of the majority Khmer population in Cambodia violated several international war crime statutes and crimes against humanity. The Khmer Rouge former officials who were responsible were tried, convicted, and sentenced, but they were not tried solely for violations of the Genocide Convention. Not all war crimes constitute genocide, and not all genocides are war crimes, as is clear in the Genocide Convention. To qualify as genocide, a case does not require governmental acts of mass murder simply worse than anything else but rather it requires a specific kind of act. The Genocide Convention is not a war crimes convention, rather a human rights convention, approved by the United Nations in the same session as the Declaration of Human Rights, which refers to individual, not group, rights. The Genocide Convention is the only international law that applies to collective rights, which is why it is uniquely important to Indigenous peoples and other groups.

Although clearly the Shoah is the most extreme of all genocides, the bar set by the Nazis is not the standard required to be considered genocide. The 1948 Genocide Convention did not yet exist for the Nuremberg war crimes tribunal, although Raphael Lemkin, who had already created the concept, attended and lobbied for a genocide convention, influencing the tribunal members. Lemkin made clear that the convention, which he helped draft and lobbied for, should not replicate German Third Reich policies and actions, because, for one thing, he was as committed to the prevention of future genocide as to its punishment. Centuries of European monarchies, states, and people carrying out pogroms against Jewish individuals and communities led to the Holocaust. The title of the Genocide Convention is the *Convention on the Prevention and Punishment of the Crime of Genocide* (emphasis mine). The law is also about preventing genocide by identifying the elements of government policies or actions that could lead to genocide, rather than only punishment after the fact. Most important, genocide does not have to be complete to be considered genocide, nor does it have to include actual death. Forced assimilation is genocidal, forcibly removing children from their families is genocidal, creating conditions that make it impossible for the group to maintain its integrity is genocidal, all of which can be carried out without death. The Trump administration immigration policy of separating children from their parents or guardians is subject to the charge of genocide, although not likely to occur in the short term. US history, as well as inherited Indigenous trauma and that of descendants of enslaved Africans, cannot be understood and accounted for without acknowledging the genocide that the United States committed against the Native nations and enslaved Africans, both of whose descendants survive in US-claimed boundaries under conditions that constitute genocide. From the colonial period through the founding of the United States and continuing into the twentieth century, this has entailed torture, terror, sexual abuse and rape, massacres, systematic military occupations, removals of Indigenous peoples from their ancestral territories, forced removal of Native American children to military-like boarding schools over a period of a century, children stripped of languages and cultures, as well as allotment of land (that is, privatization of Indigenous territories), and from 1953 to 1974, congressionally legislated policy, the Indian Termination Act. Within the logic of settler colonialism, genocide was the inherent overall policy of the United States from its founding, but there are also specific, documented policies of genocide on the part of US administrations that can be identified in at least five distinct periods:

- the Revolutionary War period through 1832 in the Ohio Country
- the 1830s Jacksonian era of forced removals
- the 1850s California gold rush era in Northern California
- the Civil War and post–Civil War era (up to 1890) of the so-called Indian wars west of the Mississippi
- the 1950s termination and relocation period

Additionally, there were genocidal policies and practices that over-lapped those time periods, in particular, the compulsory federal boarding schools from the 1870s to 1960s. The Carlisle boarding school, founded by US Army officer Richard Henry Pratt in 1879, became a model for others established by the Bureau of Indian Affairs (BIA). Pratt said in a speech in 1892, "A great general has said that the only good Indian is a dead one. In a sense, I agree with the sentiment, but only in this: that all the Indian there is in the race should be dead. Kill the Indian in him and save the man."[18] That is the definition of genocide.

Cases of genocide carried out as policy may be found in historical documents as well as in the oral histories of Indigenous communities. An example from 1873 is typical, with General William T. Sherman, hero of the Civil War, writing, "We must act with vindictive earnestness against the Sioux, even to their extermination, men, women and children . . . during an assault, the soldiers cannot pause to distinguish between male and female, or even discriminate as to age."[19] Although Sherman demurred that the US did

not desire to totally destroy the Natives, it would be necessary if they did not comply and give up. The nearly three-
centuries-long "Indian wars" technically ended around 1880,
although the Wounded Knee Massacre, of some three hundred starving Lakota Sioux refugees, occurred a decade later.
Clearly an act with genocidal intent, the Wounded Knee
Massacre is still officially listed as a victorious "battle" in the
annals of the US military. Congressional Medals of Honor
were bestowed on twenty of the soldiers involved. A monu-
ment was built at Fort Riley, Kansas, to honor the soldiers
killed by friendly fire. A battle streamer was created to hon-
or the event and added to other streamers that are displayed
at the Pentagon, West Point, and army bases throughout the
world.

Not all the acts iterated in the Genocide Convention are
required to exist to constitute genocide; any one of them
suffices. In cases of United States genocidal policies and actions, each of the five specific acts have taken place, some
still present in current policies and actions.

The old Northwest Territory was the initial site of genocidal policy enacted by the founders of the United States. By
the time of the War of Independence that created the United States, British settlers and armed white citizen militias
had 170 years of experience in ethnically cleansing and dominating the thirteen original colonies. Employing this inter-
generationally practiced and unlimited war against civilians
and their resources, the government and settlers intensified
and accelerated those practices from 1787 to 1832 in the invasion and conquest of the Ohio Country—the Northwest
Territory— which comprised the future states of Ohio, Indiana, Illinois, Michigan, Wisconsin, and Minnesota. The
genocidal campaigns carried out by the new US Army were
resisted by a confederation of Indigenous nations, but by

1803, ethnically cleansed Ohio became a state, followed by Indiana thirteen years later, and the others following.[20] In the next period of the US, the army under Andrew Jackson pursued genocidal wars in the South against the Muskogees and Cherokees and into Spanish Florida, where the US Marines and Army mounted three major wars against the Seminole Nation between 1816 and 1858, albeit without succeeding in removing the Seminole people. And when Jackson was president in the 1830s, he ordered, and the army carried out, the forced removal of all the Native people from east of the Mississippi. During the Civil War, the Union Army forced the removal and four-year incarceration of the Navajo, resulting in the death of half their population. During the same time, the Dakota Nation was forced by the Union Army out of their homeland in Minnesota, while unarmed Northern Cheyenne were massacred in their reservation at Sand Creek in Colorado.

After the Civil War, six of the seven divisions of the US Army were stationed west of the Mississippi, where they carried out genocidal wars against the Plains and southwestern Indigenous nations, including the intentional extermination of tens of millions of bison. These troops were pulled out of the South, where they were supposed to be occupying the defeated former Confederate states to allow for land distribution to former slaves and for their political participation in democratic elections. Without sufficient US Army troops to stop them, the Ku Klux Klan made Reconstruction impossible, imposed a reign of terror, and restored the ex-Confederate elite.

But the "wild west" originated in the Northwest Territory, east of the Mississippi, not in the West. Defining the West as the site of genocidal conquest erases its origins at the very founding of the United States, when and where its leaders were intent on building world power based on land theft, genocide, and slavery, the pillars of the US fiscal-military state.

It is essential to understand that aggressive white nationalism and settler colonialism form the bedrock of US institutions and historical and continuing white nationalism—a culture of violence, a gun culture, a militaristic culture—and that genocidal policy toward Indigenous nations and descendants of enslaved Africans always looms inside the US and has been extended globally by genocidal US policies and wars in the Pacific and the Caribbean, including Central America, Southeast Asia, the Middle East, and increasingly in Africa.

Why does the Genocide Convention matter?

Although many do consider US actions and policies historically and today to fall within the Genocide Convention,
most question why the Genocide Convention matters, or
why international human rights law matters at all, regarding
international law and institutions as without having any effect, given United States' domination and flouting of international treaties and norms, as it has historically and it
continues today in its treaties and agreements with Native
nations. The United Nations itself is generally known to
most US citizens as the Security Council, in which the five
most powerful nation-states have veto power over any reso-
lution. However, the UN General Assembly is the actual
governing body that produces international agreements and
treaties. But Native nations are still here and remain colonized and vulnerable to US genocidal policy, as are descendants of enslaved Africans and Mexicans, particularly un-
documented migrant workers. International human rights
law and institutions are the only instruments available to
oppressed peoples. This isn't just history that predates 1988,
when the US signed the 1948 Genocide Convention. But the
history is important and needs to be widely aired and discussed, included in public school texts and particularly in
US law schools, in order for citizens to comprehend the
present and develop knowledge and skills to deconstruct the
fiscal-military state.

The shadow of genocide lies in the Doctrine of Discovery, which remains a fundamental law of the land in the United States, the legal framework that informs the US colonial system of controlling Indigenous nations. And the US is a nation of laws, and that's the law. But the international human rights treaties that the US has ratified are also US law. From the mid-fifteenth century to the mid-twentieth century, most of the non-European world was colonized under the Doctrine of Discovery, one of the first principles of international law that Christian European monarchies promulgated to legitimize investigating, mapping, and claiming lands belonging to non-Christian peoples outside Europe. It originated in a papal bull issued in 1455 that permitted the Portuguese monarchy to seize West Africa and enslave the inhabitants, the beginning of the transatlantic slave trade. Following Columbus's landing in the Caribbean—his enterprise funded and sponsored by the king and queen of the infant Spanish state—another papal bull extended similar permission to Spain to claim the land and enslave the people. Disputes between the Portuguese and Spanish monarchies led to the papal-initiated Treaty of Tordesillas (1494), which divided the planet equally between the two Iberian empires.[21] Protestant monarchies challenged Iberian-papal domination and staked out their own claims, but maintained the Doctrine of Discovery as their legalistic justification for doing so. Not only monarchies participated. Following the French Revolution, French republics invoked the Doctrine of Discovery for their nineteenth- and twentieth-century settler-colonialist projects in Southeast Asia and Africa, as did the newly independent United States when it continued the colonization extending from the thirteen former colonies.

In 1792, not long after US independence, then secretary of state Thomas Jefferson claimed that the Doctrine of Discovery developed by European states was international law applicable to the new US government as well. Then, in the 1820s, the Doctrine of Discovery was engraved in constitutional law by the US Supreme Court under John Marshall in decisions regarding the Cherokee Nation. Writing for the majority, Chief Justice Marshall held that discovery had been an established principle of European law and of English law in effect in Britain's North American colonies, and was also the law of the United States. The court defined the exclusive property rights that a European country acquired by dint of discovery: "Discovery gave title to the government, by whose subjects, or by whose authority, it was made, against all other European governments, which title might be consummated by possession." Indigenous rights were, in the court's words, "in no instance, entirely disregarded; but were necessarily, to a considerable extent, impaired." The court further held that Indigenous "rights to complete sovereignty, as independent nations, were necessarily diminished." Indigenous peoples could continue to live on the land, but title resided with the discovering power, the United States. The decision concluded that Native nations were "domestic, dependent nations," which means captive colonies.22 The Doctrine of Discovery was a one-sided assumption of dominion that gave the discovering European entity first rights over other European entities to land and resources of the Native nations. However, the Native people did not wish to part with their land. Preemption sanctioned European priority but not Indigenous freedom of choice to sell.23 "The American right to buy always superseded the Indian right not to sell."24

It is a troubling reality that most citizens of the United States have never heard of the Doctrine of Discovery, although it is honored annually on Columbus Day, which became a federal holiday only in 1937, the same year the Buffalo or Indian Head nickel was introduced, apparently as implicit war trophies in those dark days of the Depression. Celebrating Columbus is a celebration of the Doctrine of Discovery. The Doctrine of Discovery is so taken for granted that it is rarely mentioned in historical or even legal texts published in the Americas. And yet, the United States has used the Discovery doctrine to rationalize its colonial dominion over Indigenous peoples throughout its history, citing the Marshall court precedent as recently as 2005 in the US Supreme Court case of City of Sherrill v. Oneida Nation of Indians in denying the Oneida Nation land claim. Although this was the Republican-dominated court of Antonin Scalia, Samuel Alito, and Clarence Thomas, the Oneida case was decided unanimously, with Justice Ruth Bader Ginsburg writing the decision.[25]

The settler move to innocence

A kind of innocence characterizes the erasure of continued settler colonialism. Romanticizing settler sovereignty is a way of erasing colonialism and Indigenous nations, and is a tendency as much on the left or liberal spectrum as the right or conservative.[26] Just as John F. Kennedy's book *A Nation of Immigrants* ushered in a new liberal era, so too did his romantic rhetoric about settlers as he reached the presidency. In accepting his nomination as the 1960 Democratic presidential candidate in Los Angeles, he said,

> I stand tonight facing west on what was once the last frontier. From the lands that stretch three thousand miles behind me, the pioneers of old gave up their safety, their comfort and sometimes their lives to build a new world here in the West   We stand today on the edge of a new frontier.

Echoing Kennedy in an attempt to revive frayed liberalism, Barack Obama in his 2009 presidential inaugural address also romanticized settlers, even including enslaved Africans as settlers:

In reaffirming the greatness of our nation, we understand that greatness is never a given. It must be earned. Our journey has never been one of shortcuts or settling for less. It has been the risk-takers, the doers, the makers of things. For us, they packed up their few worldly possessions and traveled across oceans in search of a new life. For us, they toiled in sweatshops and settled the West, endured the lash of the whip and plowed the hard earth. For us, they fought and died in places like Concord and Gettysburg; Normandy and Khe Sanh.[27]

Settler colonialism is in the present, as Alyosha Goldstein observes; it is not "a relic of the past but a historical condition remade at particular moments of conflict in the service of securing certain privileges and often to symbolically negotiate inequalities among white people."[28] A deep psychosis inherent in US settler colonialism is revealed in settler self-indigenization.[29] The phenomenon is not the same as the practice of "playing Indian," which historian Philip Deloria brilliantly dissected, from the Boston Tea Party Indians to hobbyists dressing up like Indians to New Age Indians.[30] Settler self-indigenization's genealogy can be traced to the period of the mid-1820s to 1840s, what historians call the Age of Jacksonian Democracy, marked by, among other phenomena, the blossoming of US American literature.[31] The giants of the era are well known to every US high schooler who has had to suffer through American Lit classes—Thoreau, Emerson, Whitman, Longfellow, Hawthorne, and dozens of others.

Among them was James Fenimore Cooper (1789–1851), who conjured the United States' origin story in his *Leatherstocking Tales*, made up of five novels featuring the hero Natty Bumppo, also called variously, depending on his age, Leatherstocking, Pathfinder, Deer- slayer, Hawkeye. Together the novels narrate the mythical forging of the new country from the 1754–1763 French and Indian War to independence to the settlement of the plains by migrants traveling by wagon train from Tennessee. At the end of the saga, Bumppo dies a very old man on the edge of the Rocky

Mountains as he gazes east. But it is *The Last of the Mohicans*, subtitled *A Narrative of 1757*, that relates the self-indigenization myth that has endured. *The Last of the Mohicans* was a best-selling book throughout the nineteenth century and has been in print continuously since, along with a half dozen Hollywood movies, the first in 1911, plus several television series made in the US, Canada, and Britain. The most recent Hollywood production was a blockbuster that appeared in 1992, the Columbus Quincentenary.

Cooper conjured the birth of something new and wondrous, literally, the US American race, a new people born of the merger of the best of both worlds, the Native and the European, not a biological merger but something more ephemeral involving the disappearance of the Indian. Cooper has Chingachgook, the last of the "noble" and "pure" Natives, die off as nature would have it, handing the continent over to Hawkeye, the indigenized settler and Chingachgook's adopted son. The publication arc of the *Leatherstocking Tales* parallels the Jackson Presidency. For those who consumed the books in that period and throughout the nineteenth century—generations of young white men mainly—the novels became perceived fact, not fiction, and the basis for the coalescence of US American settler nationalism, the settler ideology that justified the fiscal-military state.

Daniel Boone, First Pioneer

Behind the legend was Daniel Boone, a looming real-life fig-
ure, the archetype that inspired Cooper in the creation of
his hero. Boone is the icon of settler colonialism. His life
spanned from 1734 to 1820, precisely the period covered in
the Leatherstocking series. Boone was born in the shadow of
the Appalachians in Berks County, Pennsylvania, on the
edge of British colonial settlement. He was an avatar of the
moving settler-Indigenous frontier. To the west lay "Indian
Country," claimed through the Doctrine of Discovery by
Spain, Britain, and France but free of European settlers, save
for a few traders, trappers, and soldiers manning colonial
outposts. Daniel Boone himself was of Welsh heritage, born
in Pennsylvania, but most of those who followed his migra-
tions west were Scots Irish, Ulster-Scots. The Scots Irish had
been the settler colonialists of Northern Ireland. Beginning
in the early 1600s, the British decided to force Protestantism
on the Catholic Irish. They chose to use Lowland Scotland
Presbyterians. When British colonization of North America
began, many of these Ulster-Scots chose to join. They were
seasoned usurpers of Indigenous property.

The westward migration of Scots-Irish settlers repre-
sented a mass movement between 1720 and the War of Independence. During the last two decades of the eighteenth
century, first- and second-generation Scots Irish settlers
continued to migrate to the Ohio Valley, West Virginia,
Kentucky, and Tennessee. They cleared forests, built log cab-
ins, and killed Indians, taking their cultivated land. Histori-

an Carl Degler writes, "These hardy, God-fearing Calvinists made themselves into a veritable human shield of colonial civilization."[32] Richard Slotkin finds the origin of US nationalism in the late eighteenth-century treks of these settlers over the Appalachian- Allegheny spine. Daniel Boone, he writes, "became the most significant, most emotionally compelling myth-hero of the early republic," the US American hero as "the lover of the spirit of the wilderness, and his acts of love and sacred affirmation are acts of violence against that spirit and her avatars." In the twentieth-century reformation of this archetype, promoted notably in the writings of Theodore Roosevelt and, of course, in Western novels and films, Slotkin identifies the archetypes of the "hunter" and the "farmer," or "breeder," and especially "the man who knows Indians."[33] Indeed, it is rare even today to meet a descendant of the old-settler trekking culture who does not identify Daniel Boone as a direct ancestor.

Just as Boone had been hired by land speculators in 1775 to lead settlers—illegally under British law—over the Appalachians to what later became Kentucky in 1799, he led settlers from Kentucky to Spanish-claimed "Upper Louisiana," which was seized by Napoleon in 1803 and sold to the United States as the Louisiana Purchase. Boone died in 1820 in Missouri, a year before it became a state of the United States. His body was ritually taken for burial in Frankfort, Kentucky, the covenant heart of the Ohio Country, Indian Country, the Shawnee homeland for which the revolution had been fought and in which he had been the trekker superhero, almost a deity.

Daniel Boone became a celebrity in 1784 at age fifty, a year after the end of the War of Independence. Real estate entrepreneur John Filson, seeking settlers to buy property that was inhabited by Indigenous farmers and their villages in the Ohio Country, wrote and self-published *The Discovery, Settlement and Present State of Kentucke*, along with a map to guide squatters. The book contained an appendix about Daniel Boone, purportedly written by Boone himself. That part of the book on Boone's "adventures" subsequently was published as "The Adventures of Col. Daniel Boone" in the American Magazine in 1787, then as a book. Thereby a superstar was born—the mythical hero, the hunter. "The Hunters of Kentucky," a popular song that swept the nation in 1822–1828, helped elect Andrew Jackson as president by associating him with Boone, the hero of the West.[34] Yet Cooper's positive twist on genocidal colonialism was based on the reality of invasion, squatting, attacking, and colonizing of the Indigenous nations. Neither Filson nor Cooper created that reality. Rather, they created the narratives that captured the experience and imagination of the Anglo-American settler, stories that were surely instrumental in nullifying guilt related to genocide and set the pattern of narrative for future US writers, poets, and historians.

The site of the mythology that Cooper channeled was the Appalachian Mountains with their passages to the rich lands of the Ohio Valley, where British settlers were barred from making claims after the French and Indian War. The 1763 royal proclamation ordered all those who had moved into that region to return to the colonies. Defying the proclamation, George Washington, who was head of the Virginia colonial militia, took survey teams into the area to map the territory for future settlement, which by definition meant the extension and expansion of slavery. By the time he was in his mid-twenties, George Washington was already a notoriously successful slaver and land speculator in unceded Indian lands.[35] The wealthy slavers of the Southern colonies, particularly those in Virginia, were most incensed by the order since their wealth relied on accessing more and more land as they depleted the soils with intensive monocrop, non-food production for the market. The slavers also had an interest in decreasing the growing numbers of disgruntled landless white settlers, many of whom had already trekked into and illegally squatted in the Appalachian part of the Cherokee Nation. These mostly Scots-Irish settlers in the Appalachians became the mythologized settler archetype identified with Daniel Boone, claiming to be the original settlers, a self-indigenizing process. This is what has been called the "settler move to innocence."[36]

Settler claims to indignity in Appalachia

In the newest iteration of the mythologizing of white Appalachian settlers and their descendants, historian Steven Stoll first acknowledges the brutality of the forced removal of Indigenous nations from east of the Mississippi and concedes that as aboriginal nations, Indigenous peoples differed from the plight of the Scots Irish settlers. He recognizes that Native nations were uprooted and removed by the federal government as peoples, whereas the Scots-Irish were individual settlers who took what Stoll implies was ethnically cleansed vacant land and created their own agrarian civilization. Stoll then leaves the tragic past of Indigenous presence and settler-colonial violence and posits a new people—echoes of Cooper's tales—the people of the mountains who he claims resemble the peasants of feudal England who experienced foreclosure of the commons that had been provided by their lords. Yet, Stoll continually argues that there are parallels in US policy toward the "peasants" of Appalachia and the experience of Native nations. He writes,

> Both groups were cast as degenerate races with no capacity for historical progress. Neither Scots Irish cattle herders nor Chickasaw maize gardeners could be brought into the circulation of capital without shedding their rootedness in locality and their household sufficiency. Indian territorial sovereignty

conflicted with the expansion of cotton and slavery. Mountaineer kinship made some of the same kinds of claims on the landscape as homeplace. Neither group made much sense to an emerging conception of land as a commodity. Most of all, perhaps, both underwent an intellectual dispossession that preceded the one that actually took away the land.37

Stoll portrays the white, mostly Scots Irish settlers in the middle and southern Appalachians as subsistence agrarians and hunters. He concedes that they engaged in market exchange, selling livestock and lumber, but claims that they did not become dependent on the cash and credit economy that dominated the rest of the United States. He characterizes them as "swiddeners," an anthropological term indicating slash and burn agriculture, another Indigenous marker. After drawing a picture of this near-idyllic society, Stoll launches into a global history of enclosures of "the commons." Throughout the book, he applies the already somewhat romanticized histories of the feudal period of the English commons and the enclosure movement that fenced the commons and privatized the land, throwing the peasants into a surplus labor force, launching the British capitalist economy.38 Stoll characterizes the colonial settlers of Appalachia and their descendants as "peasants" who experienced enclosure with the arrival of the coal and timber industries in the late nineteenth century. The final chapter is subtitled "The Fate of the Commons and the Commoners." He compares this process to the forced removal of all the Indigenous peoples east of the Mississippi to Indian Territory and to the Dawes Act that divided all common Native land into marketable allotments. In doing so, Stoll disap-

pears the Native and bestows indigeneity upon these settlers.

Stoll didn't create the idea of self-indigenizing settlers. It
is a phenomenon that harkens back to the mythologizing of
Daniel Boone and the US origin story. Then it took new
form in the aftermath of the Civil War when Reconstruction waned, as did the possibilities of Black equality. The
mountain people as a pocket of whiteness took on a demo-
graphic category in the minds of northern elites when the
railroads brought industry into the mountains. The whiteness of the population appeared as unspoiled Americana as
opposed to the foreignness of the flood of Eastern and
Southern European immigrants arriving. The coal mining
industry took over and transformed the white settler population into heroic white miners, while labor organizing and
union militancy marked the culture of whiteness.[39] With
economic depressions and competition in the coal industry,
the West Virginia coal industry waned as did the labor
movement, leaving the mountain people impoverished,
many migrating to Cincinnati, Chicago, and other industrial centers. In the late 1960s, the War on Poverty turned attention to white poverty in Appalachia.

The Black civil rights movement in the South branched
out to the North and the entire country, radicalizing many
young white people; at the same time, the US decade-long
covert military intervention in Southeast Asia became out-
right war mobilization in 1964. Already, many on the left in
the United States and Europe were committed anti-imperi-
alists and supported the national liberation movements and
antiapartheid in South Africa. At the intellectual level, development theory—that Europe had undeveloped the "Third
World"— gained traction, so much so that the United Nations established the United Nations Conference on Trade

and Development. Out of the thinking on development and underdevelopment, the concept of internal colonization was theorized by Mexican sociologist Pablo Gonzalez Casanova in 1964 and became popularized.⁴⁰ In general, the designation of "internal colony" was racialized, indicating the impoverishment and powerlessness of African Americans living in "ghettos," as well as Mexican Americans, particularly New México. But antipoverty scholars and activists also applied it to white Appalachians, coinciding with the revival of self-indigenization.⁴¹

What set off the current Appalachian settler appropriation of indigeneity was the 1962 publication of *Night Comes to the Cumberlands: A Biography of a Depressed Region* by Kentucky lawyer Harry Caudill.⁴² In Ramp Hollow, Steven Stoll praises the book, writing, "After the book's publication, Caudill kept Appalachia before the public." In a 1967 article, Caudill wrote, "The colonialist sway in the rest of the world has ended. Only in our Appalachia does it proceed unchecked"⁴³ This was a period when most of Southern and West Africa remained under the boot of colonialism and thirteen years before Zimbabwe won independence. Caudill called white people of the Appalachians "indigenous mountaineers" who "have lived in the plateau since the beginning." He went on:

> Much of the pioneer society in this mountainous region had resided in the wilderness for three or four generations. ... They had acquired much of the stoicism of the Indians and inurement of primitive outdoor living had made them almost as wild as the red man. His "old woman" could endure harsh privations as well as the Indian squaw, and was far more fruitful. He ate the Indian's corn and "jerked" meat. He

wore the Indian's deerskin clothes. He even adopted his tomahawk, and here only, on the rampaging frontier, the white border man collected scalps with all the zest of the Choctaw brave.[44]

Appalachian scholar Stephen Pearson is one of the few intellectuals from the region to refute the concept of white Appalachians being indigenous and colonized. Exploited by capitalism they have been, but colonized they have never been. The colonial model, he writes, "maintains that White Appalachians—positioned as the region's 'Indigenous population'—are the victims of a form of co-colonialism analogous to that dominating American Indian nations. As such, the colonialism model of Appalachian exploitation calls for the 'decolonization of Appalachia.' "[45] He notes that the Appalachian case "offers an excellent illustration of how settlers can employ indigenization in late settler-colonial contexts in order to negotiate land claims and other inequalities among White settlers.

The Appalachian case shows that even in late settler colonies, Native presence remains an unsettling factor challenging the legitimacy of ongoing settler occupancy."[46] Appalachian scholars developed and refined Caudill's work, using the internal colonialism theoretical context, going further than Caudill in portraying white settlers as an Indigenous people. In 1978, scholarly articles were published in the book *Colonialism in Modern America: The Appalachian Case*, which remains a fundamental text in Appalachian studies.[47] Pearson writes that in the flagship essay of the collection, written by Helen Lewis and Edward Knipe, the authors refer to the white residents as "the indigenous population," while those of the residents who align themselves with the coal companies are designated as "natives who become colonizers of their own people." They write of the "colonizers" manifesting racism against an Indigenous population, referring to the white settler population, which the authors refer to as "the colonized." The authors analogize regional development organizations to the Bureau of Indian Affairs, claiming that the white population lives "on the Appalachian Reservation." Pearson notes that this is a comparison also made by other white Appalachian scholars. Most disturbing is that Lewis and Knipe treat the original invasion of the Scots-Irish squatters as peaceful settlements rather than genocidal violence. They portray an empty landscape that the settlers occupied, the Indigenous peoples somehow having disappeared with white settlers inheriting indigeneity and the land.[48]

In another anthology, Edward Guinan writes of the Appalachian region, "whose indigenous Cherokee integrated, educated, and nursed the exiled Celtic arrivals into maturity, wisdom, and community."[49] Julie "Judy" Bonds, a well-known activist opposing mountaintop removal, has stated that "we're a distinct mountain culture, and our culture means something. This is a culture that has been handed down to us all the way from the Native Americans."[50] David Whisnant, whom historian Steven Stoll acknowledges as one of the "historians of Appalachia whose work I read and admire," characterizes his scholarly mission as being one of Franz Fanon's "native intellectuals in a colony going through decolonization."[51] Another Appalachian scholar, Rodger Cunningham, asserts that "all native Appalachian scholarship, including mine, is like that of other colonized peoples in being engaged with history and praxis."[52] Pearson observes that "the colonialism model has allowed White liberals within the region to valorize themselves as Indigenous leaders in a struggle for decolonization—a supersessionist settler-colonial fantasy come to fruition."[53]

Razib Khan, an immigrant to the US from Bangladesh, is a writer in population genetics and consumer genetics. Although arriving as a child with his family, Khan finds aspects of the descendants of British settlers in the United States downright exotic, specifically the thirty million Scots Irish who make up around 10 percent of the US population. In an article titled "The Scots-Irish as Indigenous People," he writes, "What these people lack in cosmopolitan openness, they make up for in adherence to authentic values which can't but help earn some admiration. Substitute 'Scots-Irish' for 'Pashtun,' 'Hmong' or 'Berber' and you will see what I mean." Of course, the Scots-Irish were the foot soldiers of the British and US empires, not a colonized people, although Khan appears to be referring to their unique characteristics rather than claiming they are actually indigenous. But it does mirror the self-indigenizing settler in Appalachia. Khan clarifies that though the Scots-Irish are not "Pilgrim stock" in their length of residence on the American continent, the majority were not immigrants to the United States, they were settlers of the American colonies. Theirs was part of the founding culture of the United States. ... One aspect of Scots-Irish identity is that to a great extent it has decoupled itself from any "Old Country" consciousness. A broad swath of the Eastern American Uplands is dominated by people who give their ethnicity as American. After 250 years, they have only the vaguest recollections of the nature of their British antecedents.

Although Khan implicitly erases the original and continued existence of the actual Indigenous peoples, unlike self-indigenizing Appalachians and other descendants of original settlers, he acknowledges that the early American republic also saw the emergence of a white man's republic, where implicit white identity gave way to the expansion of suffrage to non-property holding white males as a natural right, and the revocation of what suffrage existed for non-whites based on their racial character. The Scots-Irish were a major part of this cultural evolution, being as they were generally part of the broad non-slaveholding class. They may not have had the wealth of lowland planters, but the Scots-Irish were part of the aristocracy of skin. It is true that Scots-Irish Americans are arguably among the more racist white ethnic groups.[54]

The memoir of Appalachia-born J. D. Vance, *Hillbilly Elegy: A Memoir of a Family and Culture in Crisis*, quotes from Khan's commentary positively to define his own national origin as Scots-Irish, but does not quote the part about white supremacy and racism.[55] Vance is a wealthy, self-defined political conservative, a graduate of Yale Law School, and a Silicon Valley investor. *Hillbilly Elegy* was a sensation from its release in 2016, with Oprah Winfrey's endorsement. It remained on all best-selling book lists for two years, selling a million copies. Although there were some negative reviews, it received critical attention from the conservative National Review to the liberal National Public Radio, as well as all major newspapers and media. In the fall of 2020, *Hillbilly Elegy* premiered as a major motion picture.

Vance's memoir is the second twenty-first-century Scots-Irish memoir, after that of former US Navy secretary and US senator James Webb's *Born Fighting: How the Scots-Irish Shaped America*, published in 2005.[56] Vance is critical of his Appalachian family and community, invoking the self-blaming "culture of poverty" rhetoric, but as with Webb, he is extremely proud of his Scots Irish ancestry. Like many Scots Irish men in the United States, both are proud of their service in the US Marine Corps. Webb's story is more interesting as he traces the Scots-Irish trek from the Appalachians to the Arkansas Ozark region, where he grew up. The majority of the white settlers in Missouri, Oklahoma, and Texas were also Scots Irish.

Vance writes that there is an "ethnic component" in his story, noting that ethnic differences extend beyond skin color. "I may be white, but I do not identify with the WASPs of the Northeast. Instead, I identify with the millions of working-class white Americans of Scots-Irish descent who have no college degree." He describes the entrenched poverty among his ancestors who were day laborers in the slave economy, not slavers, then they were sharecroppers, then machinists and millworkers. "Americans call them hillbillies, red-necks, or white trash. I call them neighbors, friends, and family."57 Vance characterizes the Scots Irish as "one of the most distinctive subgroups in America," with good and bad traits, the good ones being a sense of loyalty and devotion to family and country, the bad ones being dislike of outsiders or "people who are different from us." He edges toward Appalachian indigeneity, remarking apparently magically, "When the first wave of Scots-Irish immigrants landed in the New World in the eighteenth century, they were deeply attracted to the Appalachian Mountains." The term "deeply attracted" is a deeply inappropriate conceptualization of the genocidal settler invasion of the agricultural homelands of several Indigenous nations, particularly the Cherokee.58 However, actual Indigenous peoples do not exist in Vance's story, nor in Webb's.

Indigenous peoples, African Americans, and actual history do appear in a 2019 book of essays that critique Vance's *Hillbilly Elegy*.59 Appalachian historian T. R. C. Hutton writes that *Hillbilly Elegy* is "inadvertently a book about race, more so than region or class, . . . about whiteness, and the failure of American capitalism to give whiteness the natural purchase it once promised." Hutton notes that Vance implies that whiteness is the absence of race, and Vance uses the term "hillbilly," which embodies whiteness, a term rarely applied to a person of color. And, he uses "hillbilly" interchangeably with Scots Irish.[60] Legal scholar Lisa R. Pruitt writes, "Reflecting the common practice of white default or transparency, and in the fashion of Appalachian studies, Vance elects merely to imply race. Even though that race is 'white,' the use of the 'hillbilly' label permits Vance to suggest a downtrodden minority."[61]

In a review of the 2020 Ron Howard movie based on Hillbilly Elegy, writer Ellen Wayland-Smith, who is white and hails from Appalachia, asks the pertinent question: "Why does Vance's memoir strike such a sensitive national nerve?" Donald Trump had been campaigning for the presidency in the year before Vance's book appeared, using racist language and catering to Appalachians, promising to bring back the coal industry. "During Trump's vertiginous rise in Obama's ostensibly post-racial America, Vance's memoir arguably served a similar role: tacitly excusing Trump's most egregious racist dog whistles, Vance reassured readers that his hillbillies' animus had nothing to do with race."[62]

Rancher indigeneity

Settler self-indigenizing is not limited to Appalachia.[63] Under the guise of "regional studies," descendants of Appalachian and other early settlers who migrated west and settled in Missouri, Oklahoma, and Texas, many of whom trekked on to the valleys of California and the Pacific Northwest, also carry with them the sense of being of the original people and often express an affinity for their version of Indianness, being men who claim "to know Indians." Another site is the intermountain west where white cattle barons dominate, many of them Mormon, who have their own indigenous origin story blessed by their God.

On the day after the 2016 new year, an armed gang of assorted, self-styled white nationalist militias, led by the son of an affluent rancher—some Hollywood-style on horseback, most in oversized and expensive pickups or SUVs—crashed into the Malheur National Wildlife Refuge in eastern Oregon, claiming it as their land, holding the refuge center and offices for forty days. They were an exponent of an organized effort to convert all federal lands to private property, called the Sagebrush Rebellion, that began like many of the white supremacist groups during the Reagan administration. The Malheur invaders were in fairly friendly territory with white ranchers dominating the region of eastern Oregon and Washington, abutting rancher-dominated Idaho and Nevada. They run their stock on federal lands, paying little in fees or refusing to pay any fees. The leader of this armed takeover, Ammon Bundy, owner of a truck fleet business in Arizona, is the son of Cliven Bundy, who in 2014 led a gang of armed men to stop the Bureau of Land Management (BLM) officers from impounding Bundy's cattle. Bundy had been grazing his herds on federal land for two decades without paying the ridiculously low BLM fees. The unarmed BLM officers backed off, and neither Bundy nor his armed supporters were detained, and Bundy's cattle continue to graze on federal land without payment.[64]

The Malheur National Wildlife Refuge is operated by the US Fish and Wildlife Service and consists of nearly 190 thousand acres. Ammon Bundy claimed that all the land in the refuge once belonged to private ranchers and that the federal government acquired it illegally. Actually, in the nineteenth century, violent and armed white settlers and the federal government seized the land from the Indigenous Northern Paiute Nation, for whom the land was sacred. The federal government forcibly relocated the Paiutes when they resisted settler encroachment. Their residency dates back fourteen thousand years as part of the larger Paiute Nation of the intermountain area. In 1972, the 430 surviving Paiutes who had been relocated were able to obtain a federally protected small reservation on part of their original land base. The Bureau of Indian Affairs designated 771 acres as the Burns Paiute Reservation, Burns being the largest settler town in the area. The reservation did not include the already established Malheur Wildlife Refuge, which had been designated as such in 1908 by President Theodore Roosevelt in response to his ornithologist friend's request to protect the migratory birds that habituated the lakes there.[65] During the four decades since the Northern Paiute community returned to their homeland, they have developed a relationship with the US Fish and Wildlife Service to collaborate in the excavation and protection of their sacred objects that had been left in the ruins of the genocidal settler warfare that forced them out.

As the Bundy gang holding the refuge in 2016 grew in numbers, the FBI and other law enforcement presence increased as well. When one of the intruders left the site, he was detained, and when he reached for his sidearm he was shot by an FBI agent. Another intruder was wounded. In the end, after forty days of wrecking the center and grounds, opening drawers and handling the carefully excavated Paiute sacred items that were kept in the center as a secure place, they surrendered. A number of them were arrested and charged with felonies. At trial, twelve pleaded guilty and were given light sentences with probation or house arrest. Only seven received prison time. Bundy was tried by a jury and acquitted of all charges, once again victorious.[66]

Referring to the 2016 Dakota pipeline protests taking place during the same period as the trials, geographers Joshua F. J. Inwood and Anne Bonds wrote at the time,

> Nothing illustrates the fundamental contradictions of the United States settler state quite like the juxtaposition of a jury in Oregon acquitting Bundy and his supporters of the armed takeover ... while peaceful and non-violent Native Americans in the Dakotas have been subject to state-supported violence while peacefully protesting the construction of a tar-sands oil pipeline through land ceded to the Lakota through a federally recognized treaty, ... subject to tear gassings, attack dogs, have had rubber bullets fired into their protests as well as having been sprayed with fire hoses in freezing and dangerous conditions.[67]

During the takeover, Ammon Bundy was asked by a reporter about the Paiute people; his response expressed contempt for prior Paiute rights, stating a typical self-indigenizing settler refrain: "We also recognize that the Native Americans had the claim to the land, but they lost that claim. There are things to learn from cultures of the past, but the current culture is the most important."[68] In an interview a month after the occupation ended, retired Wyoming senator Alan Simpson, in response to a reporter's question about guns, said, "Without guns, there would be no West," adding that his grandfather was an original settler in the Wyoming Territory before it was a state, in 1874, two years before Custer's defeat by the Sioux and the Cheyenne nations at the Little Big Horn.[69] "The West" is a site of massive white self-indigenizing, as also reflected in the wildly popular Laura Ingalls Wilder's *Little House on the Prairie*. The self-indigenizing as first settlers is inherently genocidal with guns a central metaphor. As Simpson said in an earlier interview, "How steady you hold your rifle, that's gun control in Wyoming."[70]

Erasure

Anishinabek historian Michael Witgen writes:

> The United States imagines itself as a nation of immigrants. . . .The United States aspired to be a settler colonial power, but the presence and persistence of Native peoples forced the republic to become a colonizer. The violence of settler colonial ideology is represented not only in the widespread dispossession of indigenous peoples but also in its attempt to affect their political, social, and cultural erasure. To imagine the United States as a nation of immigrants, devoid of an indigenous population, is not only a form of erasure; it is also historically inaccurate. The United States was founded as, and continues to be, a nation of settler immigrants locked into a struggle over the meaning of place and belonging with the Native nations of North America.[71]

Criticizing US scholars for their erasure of the Indian, Mahmood Mamdani writes:

> Engaging with the native question would require questioning the ethics and the politics of the very constitution of the United States of America. It would require rethinking and reconsidering the very political project called the U.S.A. Indeed, it would call into question the self-proclaimed anticolonial identity of the U.S. Highlighting the colonial nature

of the American political project would require a paradigmatic shift in the understanding of America, one necessary to think through both America's place in the world and the task of political reform for future generations.[72]

Furthermore, Mamdani argues, regarding the conflation of immigration and settlement: immigrants join existing polities whereas settlers create new ones. "If Europeans in the United States were immigrants, they would have joined the existing societies in the New World. Instead they destroyed those societies and built a new one that was reinforced by later waves of settlement." The nation of immigrants rhetoric that avoids the dynamics of settler colonialism plays a role that "is essential to settler-colonial nation-state projects such as the United States and Israel. The political project of the settler—to create and fortify the colonial nation-state—becomes obscured by the nonpolitical project of the immigrant, who merely seeks to take advantage of what the state allows every citizen."[73]

Historian Lorenzo Veracini also distinguishes between settlers and immigrants, asserting that settlers are unique migrants made by conquest, not by immigration. Settlers are founders of political orders and carry their sovereignty with them, whereas immigrants face a political order that is already constituted. Immigrants can certainly be individually co-opted within settler-colonial societies, and often are, but they do not enjoy inherent rights and are characterized by a defining lack of sovereign entitlement.[74]

Immigrants and refugees to the United States do have the option to resist becoming settlers, although in most cases they do not know the history of the United States or the political reality. The US Immigration and Naturalization

Service policies based on exclusion make the new immigrant's life precarious, particularly for immigrants of color
entering a racial order that renders them suspect already, so
they may not want to know the reality or that they have a
choice and that by default they become settlers.

Notes

1. Patrick Wolfe, "Settler Colonialism and the Elimination of the Native," *Journal of Genocide Research* 8, no. 4 (2006): 387–409. See also Patrick Wolfe, *Settler Colonialism and the Transformation of Anthropology: The Politics and Poetics of an Ethnographic Event* (New York: Continuum, 1998). In addition to the late Australian anthropologist Patrick Wolfe's groundbreaking work on settler colonialism in Australia, New Zealand, and North America, two historians have published important books in this growing field. Australian historian Lorenzo Veracini is the author of *Israel and Settler Society* (New York: Pluto Press, 2006); *Settler Colonialism: A Theoretical Overview* (New York: Palgrave, 2010); and *The Settler Colonial Present* (New York: Palgrave, 2013). He is also the founder and managing editor of the scholarly journal *Settler Colonial Studies*. Veracini's work is global and comparative, as is Wolfe's. US historian Walter L. Hixson's book *American Settler Colonialism: A History* (New York: Palgrave, 2013) focuses on the United States, as does German historian of Anglo-American history Julius Wilm in *Settlers as Conquerors: Free Land Policy in Antebellum America* (Stuttgart: Franz Steiner Verlag, 2018). For the views of Native and Latino Studies scholars, see Alyosha Goldstein, ed., *Formations of United States Colonialism* (Durham, NC: Duke University Press, 2014).
2. Howard Lamar, *The Far Southwest, 1846–1912* (New Haven, CT: Yale University Press, 1966), 7–10.
3. David Reynolds, *America, Empire of Liberty* (New York: Penguin, 2010), xvii, 304, 458.
4. Wolfe, "Settler Colonialism and the Elimination of the Native."
5. Henry George, 1839–1897, was a US economist and journalist whose 1879 book Progress and Poverty sold millions of copies worldwide and was a longtime best seller in the United States. George argued that individuals should own the value they produce themselves, but that the value derived from land and natural resources should belong equally to all, that is, the socialization of land and natural resources rents.
6. See Wilm, *Settlers as Conquerors*.
7. Donald Harman Akenson, "The Great European Migration and Indigenous Populations," in *Irish and Scottish Encounters with Indigenous Peoples*, ed. Graeme Morton and David A. Wilson (Montreal: McGill-Queen's University Press, 2013), 22–48. See also Michael Witgen, "A Nation of Settlers: The Early American Republic and the Colonization of

the Northwest Territory," *William & Mary Quarterly* 76, no. 3 (2019): 391–98, muse.jhu.edu/article/730611.

8. Mahmood Mamdani, *Neither Settler nor Native: The Making and Unmaking of Permanent Minorities* (Cambridge, MA: Harvard University Press, 2020), 98; see also James Q. Whitman, *Hitler's American Model: The United States and the Making of Nazi Race Law* (Princeton, NJ: Princeton University Press, 2017); Carroll P. Kakel III, *The American West and the Nazi East: A Comparative and Interpretive Perspective* (New York: Palgrave Macmillan, 2013); Robert Miller, "Nazi Germany and American Indians," *Indian Country Today*, August 14, 2019, https://indiancountrytoday.com/opinion/nazi-germany-and-american-indians-Uha07e3luUCaeLq1nJP5-Q.

9. See Paul Wallace Gates, *History of Public Land Law Development* (New York: Arno Press, 1979).

10. Richard White, *"It's Your Misfortune and None of My Own": A New History of the American West* (Norman: University of Oklahoma Press, 1991), 139.

11. Victor Westphall, *The Public Domain in New Mexico, 1854–1891* (Albuquerque: University of New Mexico Press, 1965), 43.

12. See Manu Karuka, *Empire's Tracks: Indigenous Nations, Chinese Workers, and the Transcontinental Railroad* (Berkeley: University of California Press, 2019); Richard White, *Railroaded: The Transcontinentals and the Making of Modern America* (New York: W. W. Norton, 2011).

13. Raphael Lemkin, *Axis Rule in Occupied Europe: Laws of Occupation, Analysis of Government, Proposals for Redress* (Clark, NJ: Lawbook Exchange, 2008).

14. William L. Patterson, ed., *We Charge Genocide: The Historic Petition to the United Nations for Relief from a Crime of the United States Government Against the Negro People, Civil Rights Congress*, January 1, 1951, https://www.blackpast.org/global-african-history/primary-documents-global-african-history/we-charge-genocide-historic-petition-united-nations-relief-crime-united-states-government-against.

15. *Convention on the Prevention and Punishment of the Crime of Genocide*, Adopted by the General Assembly of the UN, December 9, 1948, https:// treaties.un.org/doc/publication/unts/volume%2078/volume-78-i-1021-english.pdf.

16. Patterson, ed., *We Charge Genocide*, https://www.blackpast.org/global-african-history/primary-documents-global-african-history/we-charge-genocide-historic-petition-united-nations-relief-crime-united-states-government-against.

17. "Genocide Hearings Underway in Cambodia's War Crimes Tribunal," *Deutsche Welle*, August 29, 2015, http://www.dw.com/en/genocide-hearings-underway-in-cambodias-war-crimes-tribunal/a-18699601.

18. "Capt. Richard H. Pratt on the Education of Native Americans," *Official Report of the Nineteenth Annual Conference of Charities and Correction*, 1892, 46–59, http://carlisleindian.dickinson.edu/sites/all/files / docs-resources/CIS-Resources_PrattSpeechExcerptShort.pdf.

19. April 17, 1873, quoted in John F. Marszalek, *Sherman: A Soldier's Passion for Order* (New York: Free Press, 1992), 379.

20. See Jeffrey Ostler, "'Just and Lawful War' as Genocidal War in the (United States) Northwest Ordinance and Northwest Territory, 1787–1832," *Journal of Genocide Research* 18, no. 1 (2016): 1–20; Ostler, *Surviving Genocide*. Also see Witgen, "A Nation of Settlers: The Early American Republic and the Colonization of the Northwest Territory."

21. Robert J. Miller, "The International Law of Colonialism: A Comparative Analysis," in "Symposium of International Law in Indigenous Affairs: The Doctrine of Discovery, the United Nations, and the Organization of American States," special issue, *Lewis and Clark Law Review* 15, no. 4 (Winter 2011): 847–922. See also Vine Deloria Jr., *Of Utmost Good Faith* (San Francisco: Straight Arrow Books, 1971), 6–39; Steven T. Newcomb, *Pagans in the Promised Land: Decoding the Doctrine of Christian Discovery* (Golden, CO: Fulcrum, 2008).

22. *Johnson v. McIntosh*, 21 U.S. (8 Wheaton), 543, 1823, p. 573.

23. Robert A. Williams Jr., *The American Indian in Western Legal Thought: The Discourses of Conquest* (New York: Oxford University Press, 1990), 233–86.

24. Harvey D. Rosenthal, "Indian Claims and the American Conscience: A Brief History of the Indian Claims Commission," in *Irredeemable America: The Indians' Estate and Land Claims*, ed. Imre Sutton (Albuquerque: New Mexico University Press, 1985), 36.

25. See Roxanne Dunbar-Ortiz, *Not "a nation of immigrants" : settler colonialism, white supremacy, and a history of erasure and exclusion* (Boston: Beacon Press, 2021) chapter 6 for discussion of the US cult of Columbus as original founder of the United States.

26. See Alex Trimble Young, "The Settler Unchained: Constituent Power and Settler Violence," Social Text 124, vol. 33, no. 3 (September 2015): 4, https://read.dukeupress.edu/social-text/article-abstract/ 33/3%20(124) /1/33827/The-Settler-UnchainedConstituent-Power-and-Settler.

27. "Barack Obama's Inaugural Address," transcript, *New York Times*, January 20, 2009.

28. Alyosha Goldstein, "Where the Nation Takes Place: Proprietary Regimes, Antistatism, and U.S. Settler Colonialism," *South Atlantic Quarterly* 107, no. 4 (2008): 835.

29. Stephen Pearson, "'The Last Bastion of Colonialism': Appalachian Settler Colonialism and Self-Indigenization," *American Indian Culture and Research Journal* 37, no. 2 (2013): 165–84.

30. See Philip J. Deloria, *Playing Indian* (New Haven, CT: Yale University Press, 1999).

31. See David S. Reynolds, *Walking Giant: America in the Age of Jackson* (New York: Harper, 2008), and David S. Reynolds, *Walt Whitman's America: A Cultural Biography* (New York: Vintage, 1995).

32. Carl Degler, *Out of Our Past: The Forces That Shaped Modern America* (New York: Harper, 1959), 511.

33. Richard Slotkin, *Regeneration Through Violence: The Mythology of the American Frontier, 1600–1860* (Middletown, CT: Wesleyan University Press, 1973), 42.

34. Slotkin, *Regeneration Through Violence*, 394–95.

35. William Hogeland, *Autumn of the Black Snake: The Creation of the U.S. Army and the Invasion That Opened the West* (New York: Farrar, Straus & Giroux, 2017), 19–44.

36. Stephen Pearson created the term "self-indigenization" to describe the process in this perceptive article, "'The Last Bastion of Colonialism': Appalachian Settler Colonialism and Self-Indigenization," *American Indian Culture and Research Journal* 37, no. 2 (2013): 165–84; Eve Tuck and K. Wayne Yang, "Decolonization Is Not a Metaphor," *Decolonization: Indigeneity, Education and Society* 1, no. 1 (2012): 9, https://clas.osu.edu/sites/clas.osu.edu/files/Tuck%20and%20Yang%202012%2Decolonization%20is%20not%20a%20metaphor.pdf.

37. Steven Stoll, *Ramp Hollow: The Ordeal of Appalachia* (New York: Hill & Wang, 2017), 27.

38. See E. P. Thompson, *The Making of the English Working Class* (New York: Pantheon, 1963).

39. Nina Silber, *The Romance of Reunion: Northerners and the South, 1865– 1900* (Chapel Hill: University of North Carolina Press, 1997), 14–39.

40. Pablo Gonzalez Casanova, "Internal Colonialism and National Development," *Studies in Comparative International Development* 1, no. 4 (1964): 27–37; *Democracy in México* (first published in Spanish in 1965; New York: Oxford University Press, 1972).

41. See Jodi Byrd, *The Transit of Empire: Indigenous Critiques of Colonialism* (Minneapolis: University of Minnesota Press, 2011), 117–46.

42. Harry M. Caudill, *Night Comes to the Cumberlands: A Biography of a Depressed Region* (Boston: Little, Brown, 1963).

43. Harry Caudill, "Misdeal in Appalachia," *Dissent* 14 (1967): 719.

44. Pearson, "'The Last Bastion of Colonialism': Appalachian Settler Colonialism and Self-Indigenization," 169.

45. Pearson, "'The Last Bastion of Colonialism': Appalachian Settler Colonialism and Self-Indigenization," 165.

46. Pearson, "'The Last Bastion of Colonialism': Appalachian Settler Colonialism and Self-Indigenization," 168.

47. Helen Lewis, ed., *Colonialism in Modern America: The Appalachian Case* (Boone, NC: Appalachian Consortium Press, 1978).

48. Pearson, "'The Last Bastion of Colonialism': Appalachian Settler Colonialism and Self-Indigenization," 170–71; Helen Lewis and Edward Knipe, "The Colonialism Model: The Appalachian Case," in Lewis et al., *Colonialism in Modern America*.

49. Edward Guinan, "Ashes to Ashes, Dust to Dust," in *Redemption Denied: An Appalachian Reader*, ed. Edward Guinan (Washington, DC: Appalachian Documentation, 1978), 10.

50. Quoted in Silas House and Jason Howard, *Something's Rising: Appalachians Fighting Mountaintop Removal* (Lexington: University of Kentucky Press, 2011), 144.

51. David Whisnant, "Ethnicity and the Recovery of Regional Identity in Appalachia: Thoughts upon Entering the Zone of Occult Instability," *Soundings* 56 (1973): 134.

52. Rodger Cunningham, "The Green Side of Life: Appalachian Magic as a Site of Resistance," *Appalachian Heritage* 38, no. 2 (2010): 60.

53. Pearson, "'The Last Bastion of Colonialism': Appalachian Settler Colonialism and Self-Indigenization," 172.

54. Razib Khan, "The Scots-Irish as Indigenous People," *Discover*, July 22, 2012, https://www.discovermagazine.com/mind/the-scots-irish-as-indigenous-people.

55. J. D. Vance, *Hillbilly Elegy: A Memoir of a Family and Culture in Crisis* (New York: HarperCollins, 2016).

56. James Webb, *Born Fighting: How the Scots-Irish Shaped America* (New York: Broadway, 2005).

57. Vance, *Hillbilly Elegy*, 2–3.

58. Vance, *Hillbilly Elegy*, 3–4.

59. Anthony Harkins and Meredith McCarroll, eds., *Appalachian Reckoning to Hillbilly Elegy* (Morgantown: West Virginia University Press, 2019).

60. T. R. C. Hutton, "Hillbilly Elitism," in Harkins and McCarroll, *Appalachian Reckoning to Hillbilly Elegy*, 28.

61. Lisa R. Pruitt, "What Hillbilly Elegy Reveals About Race in Twenty- First-Century America," in Harkins and McCarroll, *Appalachian Reckoning to Hillbilly Elegy*, 109.

62. Ellen Wayland-Smith, "The Mythic Whiteness of the Hillbilly," *Boston Review,* November 20, 2020, http://bostonreview.net/arts-society/ellen-wayland-smith-mythic-whiteness-hillbilly.

63. For another example of settler-colonial self-indigenization in New Mexico, see Dunbar-Ortiz, Roxanne, *Not "a nation of immigrants" : settler colonialism, white supremacy, and a history of erasure and exclusion,* chapter 5,

64. Peter Walker, *Sagebrush Collaboration: How Harney County Defeated the Takeover of the Malheur Wildlife Refuge* (Corvallis: Oregon State University Press, 2018), 2–3; Jacqueline Keeler, *Standoff: Standing Rock, the Bundy Movement, and the American Story of Sacred Lands* (Salt Lake City, UT: Torrey House Press, 2021); see also Alyosha Goldstein, "By Force of Expectation: Colonization, Public Lands, and the Property Relation," *UCLA Law Review* 65, 2018; online symposium, https://www.academia.edu/36047291/_By_Force_of_Expectation_Colonization_Public_Lands_and_the_Property_Relation.

65. Walker, *Sagebrush Collaboration*, 92–97.

66. Joshua F. J. Inwood and Anne Bonds, "Property and Whiteness: The Oregon Standoff and the Contradictions of the U.S. Settler State," *Space and Polity* 21, no. 3 (2017): 1, https://www.tandfonline.com/doi/full/10.1080/13562576.2017.1373425.

67. Inwood and Bonds, "Property and Whiteness," 12.

68. Walker, *Sagebrush Collaboration*, 45.

69. Ted Koppel, "Guns, a Family Affair," *CBS Sunday Morning*, March 13, 2016, http://www.cbsnews.com/ news/guns-a-family-affair.

70. Transcript: "Face to Face with Alan Simpson," *CBS News*, February 23, 2012, http://www.cbsnews.com/news/transcript-face-to-face-with-alan-simpson.

71 Witgen, "A Nation of Settlers," 398.

72. Mahmood Mamdani, "Settler Colonialism: Then and Now," *Critical Inquiry* 41, no. 3 (Spring 2015): 602–3, https://www.jstor.org/stable/10.1086/680088. This text is a revised version of the *Edward Said Lecture*, Princeton University, December 6, 2012, https://mediacentral.princeton.edu/media/Settler+ColonialismA+Then+and+Now%2C+Mahmood+Mamdani/0_crzrp53l.

73. Mamdani, *Neither Settler nor Native*, 20–21.

74. Lorenzo Veracini, *Settler Colonialism: A Theoretical Overview* (New York: Palgrave Macmillan, 2010), 3.

www.ingramcontent.com/pod-product-compliance
Lightning Source LLC
Chambersburg PA
CBHW070817280326
41934CB00012B/3209